THE NEZ PERCE

A TRUE BOOK®

by

Stefanie Takacs

Children's Press®
A Division of Scholastic Inc.

New York Toronto London Auckland Sydney
Mexico City New Delhi Hong Kong

A young Nez Perce traditional dancer at a powwow in the Wallowa Valley

Reading Consultant
Jeanne Clidas, Ph.D.
*National Reading Consultant
and Professor of Reading,
SUNY Brockport*

Content Consultant
Carole Simon-Smolinski
*Pacific Northwest Historian
Northwest Historical
Consultants*

Library of Congress Cataloging-in-Publication Data

Takacs, Stefanie.
    The Nez Perce / by Stefanie Takacs.— 1st American ed.
        p. cm. — (A true book)
    Includes bibliographical references and index.
    Contents: The homeland — Village life — Daily life — Europeans
arrive — The flight of the Nez Perce — Today.
    ISBN 0-516-22779-3 (lib. bdg.)   0-516-27825-8 (pbk.)
    1. Nez Perce Indians—Juvenile literature. [1. Nez Perce Indians.
2. Indians of North America—Northwest, Pacific.] I. Title. II. Series.
E99.N5T35 2003
979.5004'9741—dc21
                                                                    2003004542

CHILDREN'S PRESS, and A TRUE BOOK®, and associated logos are
trademarks and or registered trademarks of Scholastic Library Publishing.
SCHOLASTIC and associated logos are trademarks and or registered
trademarks of Scholastic Inc.

1 2 3 4 5 6 7 8 9 10 R 12 11 10 09 08 07 06 05 04 03

Contents

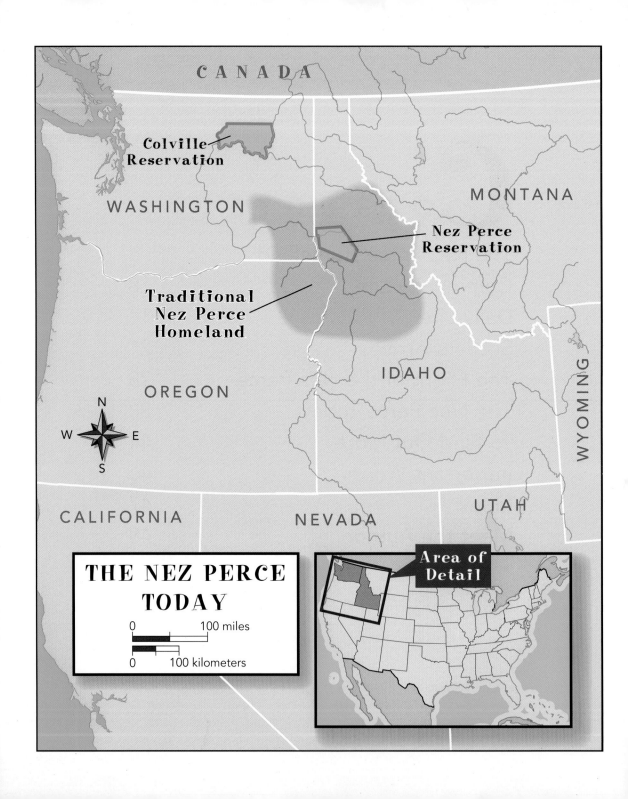

CANADA

Colville
Reservation

WASHINGTON

MONTANA

Nez Perce
Reservation

Traditional
Nez Perce
Homeland

IDAHO

OREGON

WYOMING

CALIFORNIA

NEVADA

UTAH

N
W   E
S

THE NEZ PERCE
TODAY

0   100 miles

0   100 kilometers

Area of
Detail

The Nez Perce Homeland

The Nez Perce people once lived in parts of what we now call Idaho, Oregon, and Washington. The Nez Perce are a people made up of many different **bands**. These bands all lived in the same region for hundreds of years and spoke similar languages.

5

The Nez Perce call themselves *Nimiipu* (Nee-MEE-poo). This means "the people." The name *Nez Perce* was given to them by French fur trappers who had seen Indians with pierced noses. *Nez* means "nose" in French, and *perce* means "pierced." Although some Northwest tribes did pierce their noses, the Nez Perce did not follow this custom. However, historians and many Nimiipu continue to use the name Nez Perce.

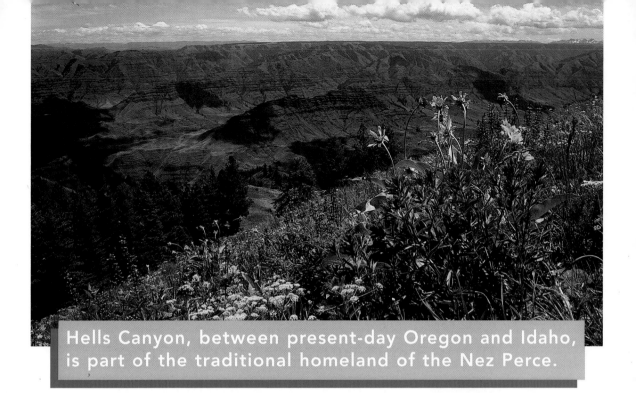

Hells Canyon, between present-day Oregon and Idaho, is part of the traditional homeland of the Nez Perce.

The Nez Perce lived on the prairies and in river valleys west of the Bitterroot Mountains and east of the Blue Mountains. Near the rivers called the Snake, Clearwater, Salmon, Wallowa, Grande Ronde, and Imnaha, the Nez Perce made their homes.

Community Life

In the cold winter months, the Nez Perce lived in small villages along streams and rivers. Their **traditional** dwellings were A-shaped longhouses covered with reed mats. A longhouse might house several families. Later, their longhouses were built more like the tepees of the Great Plains Indians and

A Nez Perce winter dwelling in the early 1900s (above) and a Nez Perce summer encampment near Lapwai, Idaho, in the 1800s (right)

were covered with animal hides or canvas.

During the summer, the Nez Perce moved to higher, mountainous areas, where they lived in **temporary**, tepeelike dwellings that were easy to move.

Each Nez Perce village had its own leader, or headman. In some villages, the role of headman was passed from father to son. In other villages, an elder of great ability earned the honor.

The headmen of neighboring villages met with each other regularly. Together, the groups of villages formed small bands of people. Each band had its own territory and was known by the name of the closest river or stream.

A Nez Perce council meeting in the 1800s

The largest village in the band would have at least two headmen. These headmen and those from the other villages formed a council that met to make decisions for the band.

Council members relied on tradition, common sense, and the **guidance** of spirits to make their decisions. The Nez Perce believed that many spirits existed in the world. These spirits gave them instruction and knowledge.

A person's first contact with the spirit world came in late childhood. At about the age of fourteen, a Nez Perce youth went on a "vision quest." This was a time to go alone into nature and talk with the spirit world.

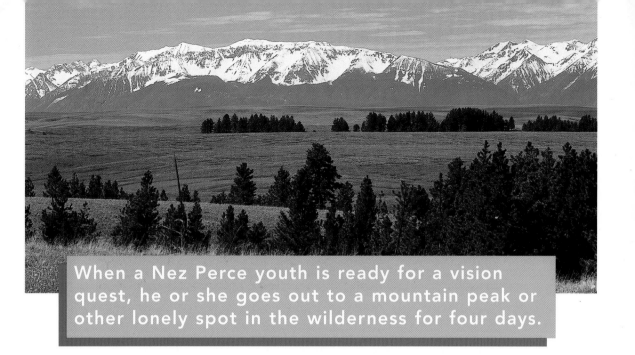

When a Nez Perce youth is ready for a vision quest, he or she goes out to a mountain peak or other lonely spot in the wilderness for four days.

The vision quest usually lasted about four days. During this time, the child had no food, water, or shelter. The Nez Perce believed that these conditions helped bring the spirits to them. Once a child saw a spirit, that spirit, or *weyekin*, guided him or her throughout life.

Daily Life

Men and women in Nez Perce villages had separate responsibilities. Among the women's jobs were making baskets and bags for carrying food and clothing. These were made from hemp and other plants. Sometimes, the **hemp** was woven together with brightly

dyed corn husks to make beautifully patterned bags.

The Nez Perce often traded these bags to tribes of the Great Plains for such goods as

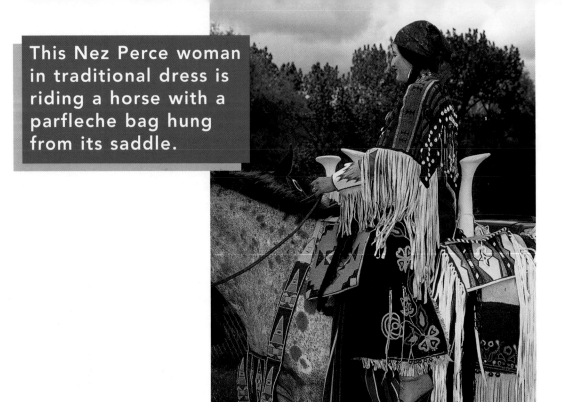

robes and hand-painted leather bags called *parfleche* (par-FLESH). The Nez Perce also made their own parfleche.

Nez Perce women and children also gathered and **preserved** roots, berries, and plants. These foods could be found in the woods and meadows. Camas bulbs, which grew in the high meadows, were a major part of the Nez Perce diet.

As this statue shows (left), Nez Perce women taught their children how to dig bulbs for food, including those of the camas lily (below).

Women prepared the meat the men brought back from hunting trips. They knew how to use all parts of an animal—nothing was wasted. They used the meat as food and the fur to make warm clothing and blankets. Dried animal hides were used to make clothing, shoes, parfleche, and tepee covers.

Nez Perce men did the fishing and hunting. From early spring through summer, they fished for salmon in the rivers and streams. In late summer, the men crossed the Bitterroot Mountains to the

Great Plains. There they hunted buffalo and other game. They made many trails through the mountains, including the famous Lolo Trail, also called the Road to Buffalo Country.

The Appaloosa

Horses were brought to the Americas by Spanish explorers in the 1600s. By the 1700s, horses roamed across most of North America. The Nez Perce quickly realized the value of having horses. Horses allowed them to expand their trade network and to chase down buffalo more easily.

The Nez Perce were excellent horsemen. They bred strong, fast horses. At one time, the Nez Perce horse herd was one of the largest herds in North America. Many people credit the Nez Perce with having created the famous spotted breed known as the Appaloosa (A-pa-LOO-sa).

Settlers Arrive

Before the 1800s, Nez Perce lands were unexplored by white people. This changed in 1804, when President Thomas Jefferson sent two explorers to the Northwest to find a water route across North America. Their names were Meriwether Lewis and William Clark.

A statue depicting Lewis and Clark meeting the Nez Perce

In 1805, after crossing the wilderness of the Bitterroot Mountains, the **expedition** wandered into Nez Perce territory in what is now Idaho. Lewis and Clark and their men were starving and exhausted. The Nez Perce saved their lives and helped them build canoes for the rest of their journey to the Pacific Ocean. Lewis and Clark left their horses behind in the care of the Nez Perce. When they returned in 1806, Lewis and Clark stayed with the Nez Perce for several weeks.

Before long, more people from the east traveled to where the Nez Perce lived. First came fur traders. Then came missionaries, people who wanted to teach the Nez Perce and other native people new religious beliefs.

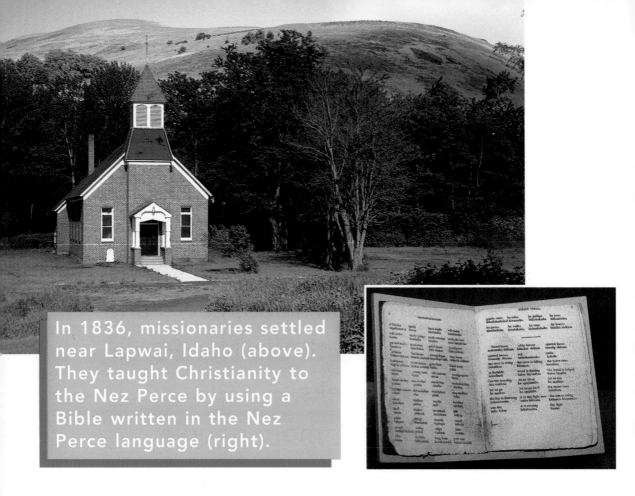

In 1836, missionaries settled near Lapwai, Idaho (above). They taught Christianity to the Nez Perce by using a Bible written in the Nez Perce language (right).

The Nez Perce welcomed the missionaries, hoping to learn more about them. Cayuse Indians who lived 100 miles (161 kilometers) to the west, however, had problems with the white settlers. The settlers brought new diseases to their area, and the Cayuse became very sick. They began to wonder if the settlers were trying to kill them with these diseases.

Some Cayuse attacked and killed a group of missionaries, thinking that this would scare settlers away. Instead, it caused problems for all the American Indians of the region. The United States government

Even when the U.S. government began eyeing the lands of many Northwest tribes, the Nez Perce remained peaceful. This 1853 illustration shows a Nez Perce hunting party talking with a government land surveyor.

started taking land away from many of the Indian peoples. They sent soldiers to the area. There was fighting between soldiers and some tribes as the U.S. government tried to keep the Indians under their control.

In 1855, the Nez Perce signed a treaty with the U.S. government. The Nez Perce agreed to sell the government a small part of their land in exchange for the guarantee that most of their traditional homeland would be set aside as a **reservation** for the Nez Perce.

The arrival of the Nez Perce at the Walla Walla Treaty of 1855

The Flight of the Nez Perce

When gold was found on the land in the 1860s, the situation changed quickly. Soon, many white miners arrived in the area. Because the earliest gold fields were outside the reservation, the Nez Perce let the miners stay.

In 1863, the Clearwater River bands of the Nez Perce signed

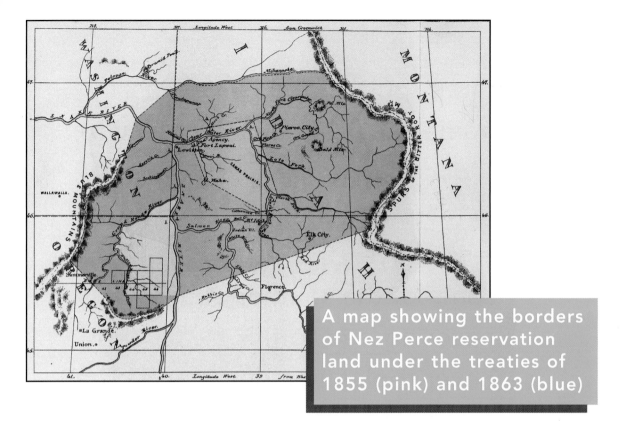

A map showing the borders of Nez Perce reservation land under the treaties of 1855 (pink) and 1863 (blue)

a new treaty with the U.S. government. The government promised them money in exchange for allowing miner and settlers access to Nez Perce lands. With this treaty, the Nez Perce lost more than three-fourths of their original homeland. Their reservation was reduced to a tiny piece of land in Idaho.

However, the Nez Perce from some of the southern bands never agreed to this treaty and never took any money for it. The leader of one of these bands, a man named Joseph, said the treaty did not apply to them. He did not believe the Nez Perce should give up their lands.

In 1871, Joseph died. His son, Hin-ma-toe-yah-laht-khit, became chief of the Wallowa

Band. He was known as Chief Joseph. Chief Joseph agreed that his band should not honor the 1863 treaty. He said that he and his people would not leave Oregon to move to the reservation in Idaho.

In 1877, the government said that all bands living off the Idaho reservation had to move onto it within thirty days or face war. Chief Joseph knew he had no choice—he did not want to see his people die. He and his followers began to move.

Along the way, however, some angry young men from his band attacked a group of white settlers who had earlier mistreated them. When other settlers and the military attempted to punish them, the Nez Perce knew that

the war they had tried to avoid had started.

At first, the Nez Perce hoped that they would have to go only as far as Montana to be safe. When they found out that 2,000 U.S. soldiers were following them, they knew they had to travel farther. The group of 500 women, children, and elderly tribal members, as well as 250 warriors, moved on. Their goal was to reach the Canadian border and freedom.

As they were **pursued**, the Nez Perce won several fierce battles, but the U.S. Army finally trapped them in Montana's Bear Paw Mountains. The army had chased the Nez Perce for four months and across more than 1,600 miles (2,574 km). Chief Joseph, the only

An illustration showing the U.S. Army cornering the Nez Perce in Montana's Bear Paw Mountains

remaining head chief, finally surrendered. He did not want to see his people suffer anymore.

The U.S. government promised Chief Joseph that he and his people would be taken to the reservation in Idaho. Instead, however, the army sent them to

Kansas and then to Indian Territory (Oklahoma), where many of them became sick and died.

Although his people had been cheated, Chief Joseph did not give up trying to get his people's land back. He even met with U.S. President Rutherford B. Hayes. Afterward, the army let some of the Nez Perce go to the reservation in Idaho. In 1885, Chief Joseph and 150 other Nez Perce were moved to a reservation in

This photograph (left) of Chief Joseph and several family members was taken during their stay in Kansas. Chief Joseph was never allowed to return to his home in the Wallowa Valley (above).

Washington State. Chief Joseph was never allowed to return to his homeland in the Wallowa Valley. He died in Washington in 1904.

The Nez Perce Today

Today, more than three thousand people are members of the Nez Perce tribe. Many of them live on the Nez Perce Reservation in Idaho or on the Colville Reservation in Washington. There are also Nez Perce communities in British Columbia, Canada.

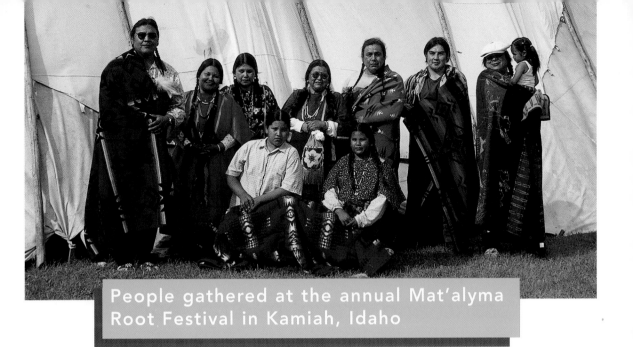

People gathered at the annual Mat'alyma Root Festival in Kamiah, Idaho

The Nez Perce are governed by a nine-member tribal council located in Lapwai, Idaho. The council makes decisions about reservation life and tribe-owned businesses.

In many ways, the Nez Perce live just like any other Americans.

They wear modern clothes, eat the same popular foods, and drive the same cars. Many people on the reservation work at jobs in farming, construction, sand-and-gravel mining, and timber and forestry. In addition, the Nez Perce operate gaming facilities and fish **hatcheries**.

At the same time, the Nez Perce proudly preserve their traditions and beliefs. They pass their history on to their children through stories and fables. Nez Perce **culture** is

People inside a traditional longhouse celebrating the birthday of a Nez Perce elder (top) and the dancing arena at the annual Tamkaliks Celebration in Wallowa (bottom)

also celebrated at **powwows,** ceremonies, and feasts.

Today, very few Nez Perce speak their original language, Sahaptin. To help preserve the language, it is now taught at the tribe's elementary school and in adult-education classes on the Nez Perce Reservation. It is also taught at a nearby state college.

Although Chief Joseph's work ended nearly a century ago, the Nez Perce have not stopped their struggle to get their land back. They continue to fight legally for their history to be protected and their treaty rights honored. In 1992, a Nez Perce

In 1997, the Nez Perce celebrated regaining a piece of land in northeastern Oregon. It was the first time the tribe had returned to Oregon since being driven out of the Wallowa Valley in 1877.

elder named Horace Axtell won a legal battle to have the Bear Paw Mountain battleground declared a historic site. Now, the place where Chief Joseph surrendered to the U.S. Army is protected as a historic landmark.

To Find Out More

Here are some additional resources to help you learn more about the Nez Perce:

 **Books**

Davis, Lucile. **Chief Joseph of the Nez Perce.** Bridgestone Books, 1998.

Lassieur, Allison. **The Nez Perce Tribe.** Bridgestone Books, 2000.

Murdoch, David. **Eyewitness Book of North American Indians.** Dorling Kindersley, 2000.

Ryan, Marla Felkins, **Nez Perce (Tribes of North America).** Blackbirch Marketing, 2002.

Stewart, Gail B. **The Appaloosa Horse.** Capstone Press, 1995.

Wells, Charles A. **A Historical Album of Oregon.** Millbrook Press, 1995.

44

Organizations and Online Sites

The Appaloosa

http://www.appaloosa.com/general/history.htm

Check out this website to read about the Appaloosa horse and its history.

Idaho State Historical Society

http://www.idahohistory.net/

This site includes information about the Nez Perce in Idaho. Search the site under "Nez Perce."

Nez Perce National Historic Park

http://nezperce.areaparks.com/parkmaps.html

This website provides maps and information about the Nez Perce National Historic Park.

Nez Perce National Historic Trail

http://www.fs.fed.us/npnht/

This site tells all about the 1877 flight of the Nez Perce from their homelands while pursued by U.S. Army troops.

Nez Perce Tribe Web Site

http://www.nezperce.org/Main.html

This is the official site of the Nez Perce. It provides lots of information on the Nez Perce, as well as links to related subjects.

45

Important Words

bands small groups of people

culture customs and habits of a group of people

expedition journey made for a specific purpose

guidance advice or supervision

hatcheries places where fish eggs are hatched

hemp plant with tough, strong fibers

powwows American Indian social gatherings or fairs

preserved dried or otherwise prepared for later use

pursued followed, chased

reservation tract of land reserved for a special purpose

temporary occurring for a short time

traditional handed down from one generation to the next

46

Index

Meet the Author

Stefanie Takacs has worked in social services, youth education and programming, and educational publishing. She has written numerous educational books on reading-test preparation and Native American peoples. Stefanie holds a bachelor's degree in liberal arts and a master's degree in educational psychology.

Experiencing new cultures is part of Stefanie's life. She has lived in Africa, South America, and the United States. She has also traveled extensively through the United Kingdom and Europe. These days Stefanie can be found in the Bronx, New York, or in the Litchfield Hills of Connecticut, where she enjoys gardening, reading, writing, running, painting and drawing, and being with her family.

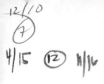

12/10

⑦

4/15 ⑫ 11/16